CHRIST FORMED IN THE SOUL

CHRIST FORMED IN THE SOUL

The Only Foundation of
Hope for Eternity

᪳

selections from
Rise and Progress of Religion in the Soul:
SELF-DEDICATION TO GOD
DO I GROW IN GRACE?
THE WELL-SPENT DAY

᪳

an extract from a letter:
FAMILY WORSHIP

REV. PHILIP DODDRIDGE, D.D.

CURIOSMITH
MINNEAPOLIS

Published by Curiosmith.
Minneapolis, Minnesota.
Internet: curiosmith.com.

The text of the sermon "Christ Formed in the Soul" is from *The Works of Philip Doddridge*, Volume III, published by W. J. and J. Richardson, R. Baldwin, G. And J. Robinson, T. and C. Rivington, Otridge and Son, J. Mathews, Ogilvy and Son, J. Scatcherd, J. Walker, Cuthell and Martin, Darton and Harvey, J. Nunn, Lackington and Co., Vernor and Hood, C. Law, Longman and Rees, T. Hurst, J. Mawman, and J. Higham, in 1804. Additions are from the American Tract Society version of the nineteenth century.

The texts used for "The Well Spent Day," "Do I Grow in Grace?" and "Self Dedication to God" are from THE AMERICAN TRACT SOCIETY published as tracts numbers 55, 232, and 407 respectively in the nineteenth century, and are extracts from *The Rise and Progress of Religion in the Soul* by Philip Doddridge.

"Family Worship," is extracted from a letter – "A Plain and Serious Address to the Master of a Family," Northampton, dated Dec. 20, 1749.

The "Guide to the Contents" was added to this edition by the publisher.

ISBN 9781946145215

GUIDE TO THE CONTENTS

Christ Formed in the Soul,
the Only Foundation of Hope for Eternity
by Rev. Philip Doddridge, D.D.

My little children, of whom I travail in birth again, until Christ be formed in you.—GALATIANS 4:19.

I t was the unhappy case of Agrippa, that though *almost*, he was *only* almost, persuaded to be a Christian;[1] and I fear it is now the case of many, and particularly of many young persons, who have enjoyed the advantages of a religious education. I believe it is difficult to find any among them who have not been brought, at some time, under serious impressions. With regard to the internal operations of the Blessed Spirit, as well as external means, the morning of life is generally to them, in a peculiar sense, the day of their visitation; and they often seem to know it, and in some measure to improve it: but in too many instances, we find their goodness as a morning cloud, and as the early dew, which soon passes

1 Acts 26:28.

away.[1] The blossoms open fair and beautiful, and give a very agreeable prospect of plentiful fruits of holiness in the life; but too often, when storms of temptation and corruption arise, the goodly appearance is laid in ruins; the blossoms do as it were, fall to the ground, and leave the tree blasted and naked, or at best, covered only with the leaves of an external profession, which, however green and flourishing they may for the present be, will not at last secure it from being "cut down, and cast into the burning."[2] Though they for a while had escaped the pollutions of the world through lust, they are afterwards entangled and subdued; and the consequence is, they prove a scandal to religion, and a discouragement to others, till, in the end, they bring aggravated destruction on themselves; so that on the whole, as the apostle observes, "it had been better for them not to have known the way of righteousness, than" thus, "after they have known it, to turn aside from the holy commandment."[3]

This may be in a great measure owing to the mutability of human nature in general, and particularly to the levity and inconsistency of youth, in conjunction with the force of those temptations of life which continually surround and press upon them. Yet I apprehend this is not all, but that it is, in part

1 Hosea 6:4.
2 John 15:6.
3 2 Peter 2:21.

to be charged on something defective, even in their best days, on their resting in something short of real religion, and a true saving change. Solomon had seen reason to say, There is a way that seemeth right to a man, but the end thereof are the ways of death,[1] and I believe every considerate person will be ready to own, that in order to prevent so fatal a delusion, and all the train of mischiefs which may follow upon it, great care should be taken in stating this important question; "What is the true and solid basis, on which we may securely ground our eternal hopes?" It is a question of the highest importance, and the most universal concern, both to the aged and the young; so that I trust I need not offer any apology for complying with the request of a pious and judicious friend, who recommended this subject to our consideration, at this time and on this occasion.

In prosecution of this design, I have made choice of these words of the apostle, which I have now been reading, and which may, without offering any violence to them, be very fairly and naturally accommodated to the present purpose.

It is plain, from many passages in this epistle, that the great apostle, who had planted the Christian church among the Galatians, had reason to fear, that many, who were by profession its members, were not sufficiently established in their holy faith.

1 Proverbs 14:12.

It is probable, that he himself had an opportunity
of making but a short stay among them; and, partly
through their own negligence and prejudices, and
partly through the artful attempts of false teachers
in the absence of St. Paul, they appear to have fallen
into a set of notions, and a conduct, which tended
not only to impair the glory, but to subvert the very
foundation, of the gospel, and with it the foundation of their own eternal hopes. Of this the apostle
does, in a very awful manner, admonish them. He
tells them, in the very beginning of his epistle, that
he marvelled that they were so soon removed from
him that called them, (and from the principles he
had taught them) into another gospel.[1] And afterwards he used these very free and emphatic words:
O foolish Galatians, who hath bewitched, or
enchanted you, that you should not obey the truth?
Are you so foolish? having begun in the Spirit (having professed to embrace the gospel, and shown the
appearances of some common zeal for it), can you
now hope to be made perfect by the flesh, or by the
ritual and carnal observances of the Mosaic institu-
tion? Is it thus that you disgrace all you have done,
and all you have borne for Christ? Have you then
suffered so many things in vain?[2] On the whole,
he tells them, he was ready to apprehend that all
the agreeable hopes, he had at once entertained

1 Galatians 1:6.
2 Galatians 3:1–4.

concerning them, would be buried in everlasting disappointment, and that it would appear, he had bestowed upon them labor in vain.[1] Thus did he stand in doubt of them;[2] and that doubt pierced his heart with the most tender concern, and brought upon him, as it were a second time, those pangs of soul which he had felt on their account, when he saw them in all the ignorance and wickedness of their gentile state. He was hardly more solicitous that they might be turned from dumb idols to the living GOD, than he was now, that they might give convincing evidences that CHRIST was formed in them, *i.e.* that they had cordially received and digested the gospel, and that their hearts were delivered into the mold of it;[3] which it did not appear they were, while they were thus making void the grace of GOD, and the righteousness of faith, by adhering to the foolish and pernicious doctrine of the necessity of seeking their justification, in part at least, by the observation of the Mosaic law.

This seems to be the most natural sense of the words of the text, where such a latitude of expression is used, as the apostle elsewhere seems to study, on purpose to render his writings universally edifying and useful to them, whose particular circumstances in life are widely different from those of the

---

1 Galatians 4:11.
2 Galatians 4:20.
3 Romans 6:17.

persons to whom they were originally addressed.

As to the introductory words, "my little children," we cannot imagine they refer to the age of those to whom the apostle wrote. The evident design of them is, to express that kind of parental tenderness which he entertained for them, like that which a mother has for an infant with which she travails in birth. "My little children, of whom I travail in birth again, till CHRIST be formed in you."

It would be easy to multiply observations from the words. I might especially take occasion to show—that it is possible, those that once seemed very hopeful, and still maintain an external profession, may appear, after all, in such dangerous circumstances, that judicious ministers, and other Christian friends, may be thrown into a great deal of perplexity and agony on their account—and that the great thing necessary to establish their safety, and the comfort of those concerned for them, is, that the LORD JESUS CHRIST be formed in them.

That I may more particularly illustrate and improve the text, and take in what is most important in these remarks, I will,

I. Consider several things, on which men are ready to build a false confidence, which will bring them into danger, and their judicious friends into perplexity upon their account.

II. I will endeavor to show you, what is the only solid foundation of their own hopes, and the joys of others with regard to them; which is here expressed by Christ formed in them. And then,

III. I shall conclude with some more particular improvement, in proper inferences from the whole.

These are plainly matters of *universal importance,* but as I am now peculiarly addressing myself to young persons, I shall endeavor to fix on those thoughts which may be most remarkable suitable to them: for I am much more concerned that my discourse may be useful, than that it may be critically regular and exact. I hope there are some among you who are experimentally acquainted with the essence of Christianity, and have received from above an "incorruptible seed."[1] There are others, to whom I must say, with the apostle to the Galatians, "I stand in doubt of you";[2] and to such, I hope, I can apply myself, in the language of the same apostle, "My little children, of whom I travail in birth again, till CHRIST he formed in you." Pardon me, if, in this instance, "I am jealous over you with a godly jealousy."[3] I would endeavor, with the sincerest and tenderest affection, and with such freedom as the importance of the case requires, first to guard you against those sandy foundations, which will bury you and your hopes in eternal ruin; and then to direct you to "the Rock of Ages," on which they

---

1 1 Peter 1:23.
2 Galatians 4:20.
3 2 Corinthians 11:2.

who build shall "never be ashamed."

I therefore entreat your serious attention, and would humbly ask, both for myself and you, the teachings of that Blessed Spirit, whose peculiar office it is, in the most efficacious manner, to show you your danger and your remedy; to aid the laboring minds of ministers, and to cause them to see with satisfaction the travail of their souls,[1] while he gives to their hearers a new birth and immortal life, by forming CHRIST in them.

I. I would caution you against several things, on which young persons are peculiarly prone to build a false confidence.

And here let me particularly entreat you, as you love your own souls, and value your eternal hopes—that you trust not to the privileges of your birth—or the rectitude of your speculations in matters of religion—or the purity and frequency of your forms of worship—or the warmth of your passions—or the morality of your conduct; for none of these apart, nor even all of them united, can, according to the tenor of the Gospel, be sufficient for your security and happiness.

1. Trust not to the privileges of your birth and education, as the foundation of your eternal hopes.

You are, many of you, the seed of God's servants, perhaps for several succeeding generations. You may be ready to plead, that you were born in his house,

1 Isaiah 53:11.

that you were early devoted to him in baptism, and have been brought up in the most regular and conscientious manner; you have been surrounded with holy instructions and correspondent examples, from your infancy and fervent prayers, both in the family and in secret, have been sent up to heaven upon your account. These are indeed signal advantages, and you may justly rejoice in them: for in these respects, you are the children of the kingdom: but rejoice with trembling; for our LORD has told us, that it is more than a possible case that the children of the kingdom may be cast out, and have their portion in utter darkness.[1] The peculiar regard shown to the seed of Abraham may, perhaps, be abused by some of you, as an encouragement to presumptuous hopes. But remember, that Ishmael was the son of Abraham, and Esau of Isaac, and yet neither the one nor the other inherited the blessing of his father. Remember that beautiful, but dreadful parable, which represents a wretched creature in hell, that could cry, Father Abraham, and yet in vain added, have mercy upon me, and send me a drop of water to cool my tongue.[2] Once more, remember those emphatical words of John the Baptist, so expressly levelled against this arrogant presumption: "Think not," says he, "to say within yourselves, we have Abraham for our father; for I say unto you, that GOD is able, of

1 Matthew 8:12.
2 Luke 16:24.

these stones, to raise up children unto Abraham":[1] as if he should had said, "The promises made to those who are the children of Abraham, respect not merely them who are lineally descended from him, but those who are the heirs of his piety and faith; for if God were to turn these stones into men, and to form them by his grace to a holy character and temper, such, though descended from no human parents at all, would, in the sense of the promise, be children of Abraham." And it were more reasonable to expect such a transmutation, than that God should acknowledge "a generation of vipers" as his people, because they were derived from holy ancestors. On the contrary, GOD directly assures us, that if the son of the most religious father forsake the way of virtue and holiness, and prove as "the degenerate plant of a strange vine,"[2] "in his trespass that he hath trespassed, and in his sin that he hath sinned, in them shall he die."[3] And surely herein the ways of the Lord are equal; for it is most evident, that a long descent from God's people is a reproach and condemnation, rather than an honor, to those who abandon that good old way in which their ancestors have trod, and as it were, cut off that entail of piety which was the care and the glory of preceding generations.

2. Trust not to the correctness of your sentiments,

1 Matthew 3:9.
2 Jeremiah 2:21.
3 Ezekiel 18:10–13, 24.

in matters of religion, as the foundation of your eternal hopes.

So various are the workings of men's hearts, and the devices of Satan, that, if I mistake not, there are some that place their confidence in the strictness, and others in the latitude of their religious opinions; but the one and the other will appear equally vain, when considered in the view now before us.

Some may possibly persuade themselves, that their condition is secure, because their sentiments are orthodox. They live, perhaps, in the midst of the unbelieving and profane, and see daily contempt and derision thrown upon the blessed Gospel, or its most glorious peculiarities; but through the influence of a good education, or from some other principle, short of true piety, they may, nevertheless, not only hold fast the faith once delivered to the saints, but even contend earnestly for it:[1] they are, perhaps, learned in the controversies of the time, and can indeed pronounce concerning them in a very rational and accurate manner.

If this, my friends, be the case with any of you, I congratulate you on the happiness of a well-informed judgment, but must caution you against mistaking it for a sanctified heart. The mystery of faith, as the apostle himself assures us, is to be held with a good conscience;[2] and in vain do you profess to retain the

1 Jude 1:3.
2 1 Timothy 1:19.

one, while you make shipwreck of the other. As precious a treasure as the knowledge of the truth is, if we go no farther than mere speculation, it will be to you "but as a talent of gold to a man sinking in the sea, which only serves to plunge him so much the deeper in ruin."[1]

There are some who err in the contrary extreme. Orthodox notions are their banter, rather than their confidence. They pride themselves in having broken the shackles in which others are confined, and in seeing through the mist in which multitudes have been perplexed. They are sensible, that many things which divide the world, as merely controversies about words; and are not much concerned about others in which there is a real difference, because they are well aware, that the fundamentals of religion lie in a very little room. They are confident of the innocency of error, and the safety of an honest mind, under those mistakes which have been branded by the severest names. A wicked life is, in their esteem, the only dangerous heresy; and morality the only thing that is worth contending about. Charmed with their own wisdom and happiness in this freedom of thought, they look down with pity on persons under the influence of a contracted education and narrow sentiments, and possibly mingle their pity with a great deal of scorn, not to say indignation. But they are indeed

1 Dr. Bates's Works, p. 938.

themselves the objects of much juster pity, if, while they glory in their freedom, they are the servants of corruption.[1]

It is certain, that the most generous speculations will no more save men of unregenerate hearts, and unholy lives, than the most rigid and severe set of notions. For notions and speculations are in their nature so far short of real goodness, that if there be nothing more than these, it matters but little what they are. Yet one cannot forbear observing a peculiar and most absurd inconsistency in the conduct of those, who think so highly of themselves, because they are possessed of this one speculation, that speculation in general is a trifle, and morality is all; as if the whole of morality consisted in bearing this testimony in its favor. I with such a character were not almost as common, as it is for men to be bigots in defense of Catholicism and uncharitable in pleading the cause of charity. If this be the case with any of you, out of your own mouth must you be condemned;[2] and we may justly apply to you, in the midst of your self-applauses, those awful words of our LORD; If ye were, in this respect, blind, ye would comparatively have no sin; whereas now you have no cloak, or excuse, for your sin.[3]

3. Trust not in the external *forms of devotion*, as

1 2 Peter 2:19.
2 Luke 19:22.
3 John 9:41, 15:22.

the foundation of your hopes for eternity.

You are, it may be, joined to some society, which not only wears the Christian name, but separates itself from many others professors, under the apprehension, at least, of a more pure and scriptural worship. You, perhaps, so much approve and esteem this worship, as to be diligent and constant in attending on the public exercises of it, not only in its stated returns, but on occasional opportunities. You fill your places here from time to time, not merely in obedience to the commands of your parents and governors, but by your own voluntary choice. And, it may be, to these you add the forms of *family devotion* morning and evening, and, possibly, a few moments of daily retirement for reading and prayer. What can such religious persons have *to fear*? No, rather, what can you have *to hope*, if, while you draw near to GOD with your mouths and your lips, you remove your hearts far from him?[1] If while you "come before him, as his people come," and present yourselves in the posture of humble worshippers, "your heart be going after your covetousness?"[2] GOD has for ever confounded such vain presumption, by declaring that the prayer of the wicked is an abomination to him;[3] and that *his* shall certainly be so, that "turns away his ear

1 Isaiah 29:13.
2 Ezekiel 33:31.
3 Proverbs 15:8.

from hearing the law,"[1] *i.e.* that refuses obedience to it. The servant that knew his LORD's will, and did it not, became justly liable to be beaten with many stripes;[2] and it is not to be wondered, if, in this sense, "judgment begin at the house of GOD,"[3] and seize first on those who affront and profane his ordinances, by making them to supersede the very things which they were originally appointed on purpose to promote.

4. Trust not to the *warmth of your passions,* in matters of religion, as the foundation of your most important hopes.

Some of you, to whom I now speak, have perhaps experienced very bitter agonies of conscience. You have been roused from the sleep of carnal security, as by an earthquake, which has shook the very center of your soul; the flames of hell have seemed, as it were, to flash in your faces; and all these mingled horrors have compelled you to cry out, "Woe is me, for I am undone! oh, what shall I do to be saved?"[4] And yet, to allude to the story of Elijah, the "LORD hath not been in the earthquake, or in the fire."[5] Consider to what purpose the inquiry after salvation has been made, and with what resolution

1 Proverbs 28:9.
2 Luke 12:47.
3 1 Peter 4:17.
4 Acts 16:30.
5 1 Kings 19:11, 12.

it has been pursued; otherwise you may be fatally deceived. The murderers of Stephen were cut to the heart by his preaching;[1] and we are sure that, if the most deep and terrifying convictions could have secured a man's salvation, the traitor Judas would have been safe, who undoubtedly felt the most violent convulsions of soul, before he proceeded to the dreadful extremity, which sealed him up under everlasting despair.

But you may have been impressed with the *sweeter* and the *nobler* passions; you have not only trembled at the thunder of the law, but rejoiced in the message of Gospel grace. The news of a Redeemer has been welcome to your souls, and the feet of those messengers beautiful, that have come to publish peace in his name.[2] You have, perhaps, been melted into tears of pleasure and tenderness, when you have heard the representation of his dying love; and when the precious promises, established by it, have been unfolded, and the prospects of eternal glory displayed, your minds have been elevated and transported; so that you have hung, almost with a trembling eagerness, on the lips of the speaker.—I readily acknowledge that such as these are frequently the workings of the Blessed Spirit of GOD upon the souls of his chosen people; and when found in a due connection with the great effects they

1 Acts 7:54.
2 Isaiah 52:7.

are designed to produce, are highly to be esteemed and rejoiced in. But remember, I entreat you, that every tear of tenderness, and every sally of joy, does not arise from so divine a spring. You might weep at a mournful scene in a well-wrought tragedy, as you have done at the story of a Redeemer's sufferings; you might find yourselves transported with a fine poetical description of a pagan elysium, or a Mahometan paradise, just as you have been with the views of a heavenly Canaan, which Gospel ordinances have presented. Mere self-love might be the foundation of such a joy in the tidings of pardon and happiness, without the least degree of renewing and sanctifying grace; as it probably was in those hearers, represented by the "stony ground," who "immediately received the word with joy, but had no root, and so endured but for a while."[1]

But, perhaps you will say, you are confident it is not merely self-love in you, for you have often found your mind impressed with a grateful sense of the divine goodness; so that, when you own it before GOD in prayer, or converse with his saints on the copious and delightful subject, your souls flow forth in love to your great Benefactor, and you look up to him in the most thankful acknowledgments of his favors.—If it be a gratitude that captivates the soul in a willing obedience, and engages you to yield yourselves living sacrifices to GOD, then is CHRIST

1 Matthew 13:20, 21.

formed in your souls, and you are not the persons to whom I would give the alarm; on the contrary, I would rather confirm your hopes, and rejoice with you in them.—But if your gratitude does not rise to this; if it rest only in some tender emotion of mind, or some transient, external expression of that emotion, I must faithfully tell you, that I fear it is only a nobler degree of that natural instinct which causes the ox to know his owner, and the ass his master's crib.[1] To find your spirit in this manner impressed, does indeed plainly prove that the day of your visitation is not entirely past; it proves you have not sinned yourselves into utter insensibility of soul; no, it may possibly, at length, through the communications of sanctifying grace, lead you on to real religion, and to eminent attainments in it: but at present it fulls far short. I have often told you, (and one can hardly repeat it too often, or insist too earnestly upon it) that there is a very wide difference between a good state, and a good frame; and that religion in not seated either in the understanding or in the passions, but principally in the will; which, in this disjointed state of human nature, is far far from being always in a duo harmony with either. So that, on the whole, those illuminations, or those affections, on which you are apt to lay so great a stress, are perhaps at best, but the preparatory workings of the SPIRIT upon your minds,

1 Isaiah 1:3.

which, if they are not improved, may leave you more hard and more miserable than they found you.

5. Trust not to the *morality of your behavior*, as the foundation of your eternal hopes.

Morality is certainly a very excellent thing, and it were scandalous indeed for any professing Christian to pour contempt upon it. Wherever this is wanting, pretences to faith and Christian experience are not only vain, but insolent and detestable. He that commits sin is of the devil; and only he that does righteousness, is righteous:[1] nor has the grace of God ever savingly appeared to that man, through whatever uncommon scenes of thought he may have passed, who is not effectually taught by it "to deny ungodliness and worldly lusts, and to live soberly, righteously, and godly." But it will by no means follow from, then, that wherever there is a sober and virtuous conduct, such a soul is passed from death to life. If the whole of the gospel be wrapped up in the rules of morality, "then is CHRIST dead in vain"; or, at least, it is in vain that the notices of his death are published to us. Beware, I entreat you, of so pernicious an error. I think myself obliged more earnestly to caution you against it, because, while the devil is attempting, on the one hand, to engage some, under the specious pretences of an evangelical spirit, "to turn the grace of GOD into wantonness,"[2] he seems

1 1 John 3:7, 8.
2 Jude 1:4.

to be ensnaring others, by extolling the virtue which he hates, in order to lead them into a neglect of CHRIST, and his righteousness, and all the peculiarities of the gospel-scheme of salvation; so that it is difficult on the whole to say, which of these devices is most destructive to the souls of men.

From my heart I rejoice to think, there are so many among you, my young friends, whose character in life is fair and unblemished. You escape the grosser pollutions of the world; you abhor brutal intemperance; you scorn the mean artifices of deceit, and renounce the hidden things of dishonesty;[1] you honor your parents and subordinate governors; you treat the ministers of Christ with respect and esteem; you are affable and courteous in your behavior to all: and, on this account, we behold you and love you; we hope, and conclude, you are not far from the kingdom of heaven.[2] But, alas! if things rest here, you will never enter into it. All these things had the young man in the gospel observed from his youth;[3] and many of you have seen, in a very large and beautiful representation, how lovely a youth was then perishing in sin.[4] He lacked *one thing;* and the lack of that was the ruin of his soul, as it will be of yours, if you are destitute of it.

---

1 2 Corinthians 4:2.
2 Mark 12:34.
3 Mark 10:20.
4 Dr. Watt's Sermons, Vol. I, Sermon 5, 6.

I know that they are especially in danger of being deceived here, who converse frequently with persons of an abandoned character; or who are themselves reformed from some gross irregularities, to which they were once addicted. Comparing themselves with others, or with themselves in a more licentious and corrupt state, they pronounce a favorable sentence, and conclude they are safe and happy: but let me entreat you, my friends, that you would rather compare your hearts and lives with that perfect law of God, which cannot be repealed; weigh yourselves in that balance, and see whether you are not *found wanting* there. Review even the upright conduct of those days of your reformation, and then say, whether there be such a redundancy of merit in them, as will not only answer present demands, but atone for your past offenses too. You will soon be confounded on such a review, you will soon acknowledge, on an impartial examination, that "the bed is shorter than a man can stretch himself upon, and the covering narrower than he can wrap himself in";[1] that neither you, nor any living, can be justified by the works of the law.[2]

I will conclude this head with observing, that the instance of the blessed Apostle St. Paul serves well to illustrate and confirm our discourse, in each of the particulars I have now mentioned—Had the

1 Isaiah 28:20.
2 Romans 3:20.

privileges of birth and education been a sufficient security, Paul had been secure before his conversion to Christianity; for he was circumcised the eighth day, of the stock of Israel, of the tribe of Benjamin, (which had not, like the rest, revolted from the house of David) and by his mother's side, as well as his father's, *a Hebrew of the Hebrews.*[1]—If the exactest regularity in religious notions, or the strictest formality in the externals of worship, could have secured a man, Paul had been secure; for he was, as touching the law, a Pharisee; he lived according to the rigor of that sect, and, both with respect to doctrines and ceremonies, "was exceedingly zealous of the traditions of the fathers."[2]—If a transport of passion in the cause of God could have secured a man, Paul had been secure; for, "concerning zeal, or with regard to that, he persecuted the church, and wasted it beyond measure."[3]—And, lastly; if morality of behavior could have done it, Paul had been secure; for, touching the righteousness which is by the law, he was "blameless."[4] In these things he was once so weak, and so wretched, as to place a great deal of confidence; but when he was illuminated, and called by divine grace, he assures us, that what things were gain unto him before, those he counted

1 Philippians 3:5.
2 Galatians 1:14.
3 Galatians 1:13.
4 Philippians 3:6–8.

loss for CHRIST, *i.e.* he most entirely renounced all dependence upon them. "Yea doubtless," says he, "and I count all things but loss, for the excellency of the knowledge of CHRIST JESUS my Lord." Which naturally leads me to the second general, where

II. I am to consider, what will be a SOLID FOUNDATION for hope and joy when all these precarious dependences fail.

This is, with the utmost propriety, expressed in the text, by *Christ formed in the soul;* which is exactly parallel to that phrase in Colossians, CHRIST in you, the hope of glory,[1] which is there mentioned as an epitome of the gospel, the riches of the glory of the mystery preached among the Gentiles. When Paul could see that the Galatians were brought to this, the pangs of his laboring mind would be ended, and joy and confidence would succeed; which is plainly intimated in the words of the text. And when you, my dear charge, are brought to it, parents and ministers may rejoice over you, and you will have an everlasting spring of hope and joy, a solid foundation, on which to build for eternity.

Permit me, therefore, a little more particularly to explain it to you; and let me entreat you to turn your thoughts inward, that you may judge whether you have been experimentally acquainted with the temper and change which I shall now describe, as signified by this remarkable expression in the text,

1 Colossians 1:27.

Christ formed in you.

Now, I think, it implies these three things—
That some apprehensions of CHRIST have taken
hold of the heart—that the man is brought to an
explicit choice of him, and deliberately enters into
covenant with him—and that, in consequence of
both these, something of the temper and spirit of
CHRIST is, by divine grace wrought in his soul. I
will touch on each of these; but my time will not
allow me to manage them in so copious and particular a manner as they well deserve.

1. To have Christ formed in the soul supposes,
that some *serious apprehensions of Christ have
taken hold of the heart.*

It evidently implies, that the external revelation
of him has not only been admitted as a speculative
truth, but attended to as a matter of the highest concern. Previous to the forming of CHRIST in the soul,
there must be a conviction that we are naturally without CHRIST, and that, in consequence of this, we are
in a most unhappy condition. And this conviction
must strike deep upon the heart; for till the evil of
sin be felt, what can make the news of a Saviour
welcome? Since, as he himself has declared, "the
whole need not a physician, but they that are sick."[1]
The man in whose heart CHRIST is formed, has seen
himself condemned by GOD's righteous law; has
seen himself equally unable to answer its demands,

1 Matthew 9:12.

or to bear up under the execution of its penalties. And feeling this to be no light matter, but the very life of his soul, he has then been engaged, with the greatest seriousness and earnestness, to cry out, "Woe is me, for I am undone!"[1] Oh, "what shall I do to be saved?"[2] I before told you, there may be these convictions and awakenings, where CHRIST is never formed in the soul; and I now add, that the degree of them may be various, according to the various tempers and circumstances of different persons: but it is most evident that something of this kind must make way for the REDEEMER's entrance, who comes to seek and to save that which was lost;[3] to bind up the broken-hearted,[4] and to give rest to the weary and heavy-laden.[5] And I the rather insist on this, because I am fully persuaded, that slight thoughts of sin, and of the misery of our natural estate by it, have been the principal cause of all the infidelity of the present age, and are daily ruining a multitude of souls.

2. The formation of CHRIST in the soul does farther imply *an explicit choice of him*, and a deliberate *entering into covenant with him*.

When such a soul hears of a REDEEMER, and of the way of salvation by him, exhibited in Scripture,

---

1 Isaiah 6:5.
2 Acts 16:30.
3 Luke 19:10.
4 Isaiah 61:1.
5 Matthew 11:28, 29.

it cordially approves the scheme, as entirely worthy of its divine author; and though corrupt nature raises up a thousand proud thoughts, in a vain and ungrateful rebellion against it, yet they are by Almighty grace, subdued and brought into captivity.[1] The man really sees such a suitableness, and such an amiableness, in the blessed Jesus, under the character in which the Gospel reveals him, that he judges him to be "the pearl of great price"; and as God has laid him as "the foundation-stone," he is, in that view, inconceivably "precious to him."[2] Far from contenting himself with applauding this plan, as regularly beautiful, and magnificent in general, the true believer is solicitous, that he may have his own share in this edifice of mercy; and that, "coming to Christ as a living stone," he may himself be one of those, who shall, "on him be built up for an habitation of God through the Spirit."[3] When he considers the Lord Jesus represented as standing at the door and knocking,[4] it is with pleasure that he hears his voice, and opens to him, and, as Zaccheus did, *receives him joyfully.*[5] He regards him as a nail fastened in a sure place;[6] on which he can joyfully fix all his eternal

---

1 2 Corinthians 10:5.
2 1 Peter 2:6.
3 Ephesians 2:22.
4 Revelation 3:20.
5 Luke 19:6.
6 Isaiah 22:23.

hopes, infinitely important as he sees them to be. And while he thus anchors his soul on the righteousness, the atonement, and the intercession of a REDEEMER, he humbly bows to his authority, as his Lord and his God.[1] It is his desire to seat him on the throne in his heart, and as it were, to put into his hand the scepter and the sword, that all the powers of nature may be governed, and all the corruptions of it destroyed by him. In a word, as he knows that CHRIST was given for a covenant to the people,[2] he deliberately sets his seal to that covenant, thereby devoting himself to CHRIST, and, through him, to the Father. Such are his views, his purposes, and his engagements; and by divine grace he is enabled to be faithful to them. Which leads me to add,

3. When CHRIST is formed in any soul, something of the *temper and character of the Blessed Jesus* is, by divine grace wrought there.

I might with ease multiply scriptures in proof of the absolute necessity of this; but it is so obvious, that you must yourselves know, how expressly it is required. You know, how plainly St. Paul has told us, that "if any man have not the Spirit of CHRIST, he is none of his":[3] and where the Spirit resides Christ dwells in the heart.[4] The same mind, or temper, is

---

1 John 20:28.
2 Isaiah 49:8.
3 Romans 8:9.
4 Ephesians 3:17.

in such an one, as was also in CHRIST JESUS;[1] and as he professes to abide in him, it is his care so to walk as CHRIST also walked.[2] On which account the true Christian is said to have "put on CHRIST,"[3] in allusion to the Hebrew phrase, of being clothed with any temper or affection, that greatly prevails or governs in the soul.[4]

It is a very pleasing, as well as useful employment, to trace the lineaments of the temper and conduct of CHRIST in his people. Our LORD is in a peculiar sense the SON of GOD; but his people are, through him, taken into the same relation: for they "have not received the spirit of bondage again unto fear," though perhaps they were once subjected to it, but they "have received the spirit of adoption";[5] and because they "are sons, GOD hath sent forth the spirit of his SON into their hearts, crying Abba, Father."[6] By this Spirit a filial temper is wrought in their souls, by which their obedience to their heavenly Father is so animated, as to be most honorable and grateful to him, as well as most easy and

1 Philippians 2:5.
2 1 John 2:6.
3 Galatians 3:27.
4 Thus we read of being clothed with righteousness, Job 29:14; Psalm 132:9; with humility, 1 Peter 5:5; with zeal, Isaiah 59:17; with cursing, Psalm 109:18; with shame, Psalm 132:18, etc.
5 Romans 8:15.
6 Galatians 4:6.

delightful to themselves. Under the influences of this spirit, the Christian desires it may be his character now, as he trusts it will be his happiness at last, to "follow the Lamb wherever he goes";[1] to follow that Jesus, who was "holy, harmless, undefiled, and separate from sinners."[2] He is indeed deeply sensible, that it is impossible for him, as his Lord did, to fulfill all righteousness;[3] and therefore, when he has done all, he calls himself an unprofitable servant.[4] Yet he sees so much of the internal beauties of holiness, so much luster and glory in the image of GOD, as drawn on the soul of man, that it is the great concern of his heart, and labor of his life to pursue it.

Nor would he only abstain from grosser enormities, and practice those virtues which are most honorable among men, and attended with the greatest secular advantage; but he would, in every respect, "maintain a conscience void of offense,"[5] and "perfect holiness in the fear of GOD."[6] He has so affectionate a sense of the riches of the divine grace, displayed through a REDEEMER, in adopting so unworthy a creature as himself to the dignity and privileges of a son of GOD, that he often cries out, in

1 Revelation 14:4.
2 Hebrews 7:26.
3 Matthew 3:15.
4 Luke 17:10.
5 Acts 24:16.
6 2 Corinthians 7:1.

raptures of holy gratitude and joy, "What shall I render unto the Lord for all his benefits towards me?"[1] Inspired with this noble principle, he searches his father's will impartially; and when he has discovered it, he obeys it cheerfully, and it is his meat and his drink to perform it. He loves the LORD his GOD above all, and loves his fellow creatures for his sake as well as their own, and entertains the highest veneration and affection for those who most heartily resemble his Father and their Father, his God and their God.

It is his prayer, and his endeavor, that he may go about doing good,[2] and be useful to all as he has opportunity;[3] that he pass through the world with a holy moderation and superiority of soul, to the things which are seen and are temporal;[4] thankfully owning every mercy as proceeding from God's paternal love and care, and serenely submitting to every affliction, as the cup which his Father puts into his hand.[5] In a word, he desires, that in all the varieties of life he may still be intent on the views of an everlasting inheritance; humbly looking and longing for that blessed hope,[6] yet willing patiently to wait his Father's time, having this constant expectation, and reviving assurance, that whether he lives, he shall

1 Psalm 116:12.
2 Acts 10:38.
3 Galatians 6:10.
4 2 Corinthians 4:18.
5 John 8:11.
6 Titus 2:13.

live unto the LORD, or whether he dies, he shall die unto the LORD; so that whether he live or die, he shall be the LORD's.[1]

This is the Christian—this is the man *in whom Christ is formed;* or, rather, these are some faint lineaments of his character: and I will venture to say, that he who cannot discern something in it, even as thus imperfectly described, which is vastly superior to that morality and decency of behavior, which arises merely from prudential views, or from the sweetness and gentleness of a man's natural temper, is sunk below the boasted religion of nature, and must take refuge in the wretched principles of Atheism, if he would pretend to form any thing of a consistent scheme. But now,

III. I must conclude with hinting at some *reflections and inferences*, which my time will not allow me to handle at large.

1. How important is it, that *ministers of the Gospel* should lead *young persons* into such views as these!

Our great and important business in life is to promote the eternal happiness of our hearers, and to lay a solid foundation of hope and joy in their souls. We have seen now what it is, and other foundation can no man lay than that is laid, which is JESUS CHRIST.[2] Here then let all our labors center.

---

1 Romans 14:8.
2 1 Corinthians 3:11.

It is the good old way, in which our fathers in the ministry went, and in which they prospered. Let us follow their steps, and exert our most vigorous efforts here. Modern refinements may amuse us in our closets, but they will never feed the souls of our hearers, nor spread the triumphs of a gospel, which was the power of God to the salvation of thousands, before they were ever dreamt of. I hope, God is my witness, that I am heartily concerned for the interest of virtue, (if by that be meant the advancement of practical religion) but I never expected to see it promoted by the most philosophical speculations concerning its nature, or the finest harangues on its innate beauties, when the name and peculiar doctrines of CHRIST are thrown off, as unfashionable incumbrances of a discourse. Experienced Christians who have tasted the bread of life, will not contentedly be put off with such chaff: and if we imagine that the younger part of our auditors may be trained up to a relish for it, we may, perhaps, succeed in the attempt; but I much fear, that success will be the calamity of the church, and the destruction of souls.[1]

2. We may learn from this, what are the most valuable proofs of *parental affection*.

Certainly, there is no reason to esteem, as such, that fond indulgence which suffers ill habits to

1 The author has taken a greater freedom on this head, as the discourse was delivered before several candidates for the ministry, for whom he had some peculiar concern.

grow up in the young mind, and fears its present disturbance more than its future ruin; no, nor yet the more prudent care of providing plentiful and agreeable accommodations, for the subsistence and delight of your infant offspring, as they advance to maturity and settlement in life. These things indeed are not to be neglected; but wretched are the children, and I will add, the parents too, where this is the principal labor. Would you express a wise and religious tenderness, for which your children shall have reason to thank you in their dying moments, and to meet you with joy in the interviews of the eternal world, do your utmost that *Christ be formed in their souls;* and let them plainly see, that you even travail in birth again, till this happy work be accomplished. But this leads me to add,

3. How needful is *the work of the Holy Spirit on the heart,* in order to the laying this great foundation?

The language of the text, which speaks of CHRIST formed in us, naturally leads our thoughts to some *agent,* by whom the work is done; and when you consider what kind of a work it is, I appeal to your own consciences, whether it is to be thought merely a human production? Were it only a name, a ceremony, a speculation, or a passion, it would not be worth a moment's dispute, whether *you* or *we* should have the glory of if. But as it is nothing less than the transformation of a corrupt and degenerate creature into the holy image of the SON of GOD, it were impiety for either to arrogate it to ourselves.

Let us therefore on the whole learn our duty and our wisdom. Let the matter be brought to a serious and immediate review, and let us judge ourselves by the character described, as those that expect very shortly to be judged of the LORD.—If, on the examination, any of you have reason to conclude that you are strangers to it, remember that the invincible battery of the Word of God demolishes all the towering hopes you may have raised on any other foundation. Let conscience then say, whether any amusement, or any business in life, be so important as to be attended to, even for one single day, in neglect of this great concern, on which all the happiness of an immortal soul is suspended. If nothing be indeed found of greater moment, apply yourselves seriously to this, and omit no proper and rational method of securing it. Consider the ways by which Christ uses to enter into a soul, and wait upon him in those ways. Reflect seriously on your present condition; constantly attend the instructions of his Word, and the other solemnities of his worship; and choose to converse intimately with those, in whom you have reason to think he is already formed. But in all remember, that the success depends upon a divine cooperation, and therefore go frequently into the presence of GOD by prayer; go into it this day, or if possible this hour, and importunately entreat the regenerating and sanctifying influences of his Spirit, which, when you earnestly desire them, the gospel gives you such ample encouragement to expect.—But if you have reason to hope that you have already received them, learn to what the praise should be ascribed; and let it animate you to pray, that through farther communications from the throne of grace, you may be made continually more and more like to your REDEEMER, till you are prepared for that world where you shall shine forth in his complete resemblance, and shall find it your complete and eternal felicity. Amen.

SINNERS INVITED TO CHRIST

Come, ye weary, heavy laden,
　　Lost and ruined by the fall;
If you tarry till you're better,
　　You will never come at all:
　　　　Not the righteous—
　　Sinners Jesus came to call.

Let not conscience make you linger,
　　Nor of fitness fondly dream;
All the fitness he requireth,
　　Is to feel your need of him.
　　　　This he gives you—
　　'Tis the Spirit's rising beam.

Agonizing in the garden,
　　Lo! your Maker prostrate lies;
On the bloody tree behold him;
　　Hear him cry before he dies,
　　　　"It is finished"
　　Sinners, will not this suffice?

Lo! the incarnate God ascended,
　　Pleads the merit of his blood;
Venture on him, venture wholly,
　　Let no other trust intrude:
　　　　None but Jesus
　　Can do helpless sinners good.

Saints and angels, joined in concert,
　　Sing the praises of the Lamb;

While the blissful seats of heaven
Sweetly echo with his name:
Hallelujah!—
Sinners here may sing the same.

JOSEPH HART

Self-Dedication to God

by Rev. Philip Doddridge, D.D.

MY DEAR FRIEND—You have felt your lost condition as a sinner against God. You have felt your need of the atoning blood of Christ. You know that blood can be available for you, only by your believing in him—trusting in him—dedicating yourself to him, through the promised aids of the Holy Spirit. To this act of dedication you are now urged by conscience, by the Word of God, and by the strivings of the Spirit. And it may be of great use to you, not only to form in your heart the purpose of surrendering yourself to God, but expressly to declare it in the divine presence. Such solemnity in the manner of doing it, is certainly very reasonable in the nature of things; and surely it is highly expedient for binding to the Lord such a treacherous heart as we know our own to be.

Do it therefore; but do it *deliberately*. Consider what it is that you are to do, and consider how reasonable it is that it should be done cordially and cheerfully; "not by constraint, but willingly,"[1] for in this sense, and in every other, "God loveth a cheerful giver."[2] Nothing can be more evident than that we, the product of his power, and the price of his Son's blood, should be his, and his for ever. If you see the matter in its just view, it will be the grief of your soul that you have ever alienated yourself from the blessed God and his service: so far will you be from wishing to continue in that state of alienation another year, or another day, you will rejoice to bring back to him his revolted creature; and as you have in times past "yielded your members as instruments of unrighteousness unto sin," you will delight to "yield yourself unto God as alive from the dead."[3]

The surrender will also be as *entire* as it is *cheerful* and *immediate*. All you are, and all you have, and all you can do—your time, your possessions, your influence over others—will be devoted to him, that for the future it may be employed entirely for him, and to his glory. You will desire to keep back nothing from him; but will seriously judge that you are then in the truest and noblest sense your own, when you are most entirely his. You are also, on this great occasion, to resign all that you have to the disposal of his wise and gracious providence; not only owning his power,

1 1 Peter 5:2.
2 2 Corinthians 9:7.
3 Romans 6:13.

but consenting to his undoubted right to do what he pleases with you, and all that he has given you.

Once more, let me remind you that this surrender must be *perpetual*. You must give yourself up to God in such a manner as never more to pretend to be your own; for the rights of God are, like his nature, eternal and immutable; and with regard to his rational creatures, are the same yesterday, today, and for ever.

I would farther advise and urge, that this dedication may be made with all possible *solemnity*. Do it in express words. And perhaps it may be in many cases most expedient, as many pious divines have recommended, to do it in writing. Set your hand and seal to it, "that on such a day of such a month and year, and at such a place, on full consideration and serious reflection, you came to this happy resolution, that, whatsoever others might do, you would serve the Lord."

Such an instrument you may, if you please, draw up for yourself; or, if you rather choose to have it drawn up to your hand, you may find something of this nature below, in which you may easily make such alterations as your circumstances may seem to require. But whatever form you use, weigh it well, meditate attentively upon it, that you may "not be rash with your mouth to utter any thing before God."[1] And when you determine to execute

1 Ecclesiastes 5:2.

this instrument, let the transaction be attended with some more than ordinary religious retirement. Make it, if you conveniently can, a day of secret fasting and prayer; and when your heart is prepared with a becoming awe of the divine Majesty, with an humble confidence in his goodness, and an earnest desire of his favor, then present yourself on your knees before God, and read it over deliberately and solemnly; and when you have signed it, lay it by in some secure place, where you may review it whenever you please; and make it a rule with yourself to review it, if possible, at certain seasons of the year, that you may keep up the remembrance of it. And God grant that you may be enabled to keep it, and in the whole of your life walk according to it. May it be an anchor to your soul in every temptation, a cordial in every affliction, and may the recollection of it give strength to your departing spirit, in a consciousness that it is ascending to your covenant God and Father, and to that gracious Redeemer whose power and faithfulness will securely "keep what you commit to him unto that day."[1]

AN EXAMPLE OF SELF-DEDICATION

"Eternal and ever-blessed God, I desire to present myself before thee, with the deepest humiliation and abasement of soul, sensible how unworthy such

---

1 2 Timothy 1:12.

a sinful worm is to appear before the holy Majesty of heaven, the King of Kings and Lord of Lords, and especially on such an occasion as this, ever to dedicate myself, without reserve, to thee. But the scheme and plan is thine own. Thine infinite condescension has offered it by thy Son, and thy grace has inclined my heart to accept of it.

"I come, therefore, acknowledging myself to have been a great offender; smiting upon my breast, and saying with the humble publican, 'God be merciful to me a sinner.'[1] I come, invited by the name of thy Son, and wholly trusting in his perfect righteousness, entreating that for his sake thou will be merciful to my unrighteousness, and will no more remember my sins. Receive, I beseech thee, thy revolted creature, who is now convinced of thy right to him, and desires nothing so much as that he may be thine.

"This day do I, with the utmost solemnity, surrender myself to thee. I renounce all former lords that have had dominion over me; and I consecrate to thee all that I am, and all that I have: the faculties of my mind, the members of my body, my worldly possessions, my time, and my influence over others; to be all used entirely for thy glory, and steadfastly employed in obedience to thy commands, as long as thou continuest me in life; with an ardent desire and humble resolution to continue thine through

1 Luke 18:13.

all the endless ages of eternity; ever holding myself in an attentive posture to observe the first intimations of thy will, and ready to spring forward with zeal and joy to the immediate execution of it.

"To thy direction also I resign myself, and all I am and have, to be disposed of by thee in such a manner as thou shalt in thine infinite wisdom judge most subservient to the purposes of thy glory. To thee I leave the management of all events, and say without reserve, 'Not my will, but thine be done,'[1] rejoicing with a loyal heart in thine unlimited government, as what ought to be the delight of the whole rational creation.

"Use me, O Lord, I beseech thee, as an instrument of thy service. Number me among thy peculiar people. Let me be washed in the blood of thy dear Son. Let me be clothed with his righteousness. Let me be sanctified by his Spirit. Transform me more and more into his image. Impart to me, through him, all needful influences of thy purifying, cheering, and comforting Spirit. And let my life be spent under those influences, and in the light of thy gracious countenance, as my Father and my God.

"And when the solemn hour of death comes, may I remember thy COVENANT, 'well-ordered in all things and sure, as all my salvation, and all my desire,'[2] though every hope and enjoyment is

1 Luke 22:42.
2 2 Samuel 23:5.

perishing; and do thou, O Lord, remember it too. Look down with pity, O my heavenly Father, on thy languishing, dying child. Embrace me in thine everlasting arms. Put strength and confidence into my departing spirit, and receive it to the abodes of them that sleep in Jesus, peacefully and joyfully to wait the accomplishment of thy great promise to all thy people, even that of a glorious resurrection, and of eternal happiness in thine heavenly presence.

"And if any surviving friend should, when I am in the dust, meet with this memorial of my solemn transactions with thee, may he make the engagement his own; and do thou graciously admit him to partake in all the blessings of THY COVENANT, through Jesus the great Mediator of it; to whom, with thee, O Father, and thy Holy Spirit, be everlasting praises. Amen."

Do I Grow In Grace?

By Rev. Philip Doddridge, D. D.

If by divine grace you have "been born again, not of corruptible seed, but of incorruptible," you will, "as newborn babes, desire the sincere milk of the word, that you may grow thereby." I would therefore endeavor to assist you in making the inquiry, whether religion be on the advance in your soul.

And here I shall warn you against some *false marks* of growth. In this view I would observe, that you are not to measure your growth in grace only or chiefly by your advances in knowledge, or in zeal, or any other passionate impression of the mind—no, nor by the fervor of devotion alone; but by the habitual determination of your mind for God, and by your prevailing disposition to obey his commands, submit to his disposal, and promote the highest welfare of his cause in the earth.

It must be allowed, that knowledge and affection in religion are indeed desirable. Without some degree of the former, religion cannot be rational; and it is very reasonable to believe that, without some degree of the latter, it cannot be sincere in creatures whose natures are constituted like ours. Yet there may be a great deal of speculative knowledge, and a great deal of rapturous affection, where there is no true religion at all; and still more, where religion exists, though there be no advanced state of it. The exercise of our rational faculties, upon the evidences of divine revelation, and upon the declaration of it as contained in Scripture, may furnish a very wicked man with a well-digested body of orthodox divinity in his head, when not one single doctrine of it has ever reached his heart. An eloquent description of the sufferings of Christ, of the solemnities of judgment, of the joys of the blessed and the miseries of the damned, might move the breast even of a man who did not firmly believe them; as we often find ourselves strongly moved by well-wrought narrations or discourses, which at the same time we know to have their foundation in fiction. Natural constitution, or such accidental causes as are, some of them, too low to be here mentioned, may supply the eyes with a flood of tears, which may discharge itself plenteously upon almost any occasion that shall first arise. And a proud impatience of contradiction, directly opposite as it is to the gentle spirit of Christianity, may make a man's blood boil when he hears the notions he has entertained, and especially those which he has openly and vigorously espoused, disputed and opposed. This may possibly lead him, in terms of strong indignation, to pour out his zeal and his rage before God, in a fond conceit that, as the God of truth, he is the pattern of those favorite doctrines, by whose fair appearances perhaps he himself is misled. But these speculative refinements, and these affectionate sallies of the mind, may exist where there is a total absence of true religion.

I would desire to lead you, my friend, to sublimer notions and JUSTER MARKS; and refer you to other practical writers, and, above all, to the book of God, to prove how material they are. I would therefore entreat you to bring your own heart to answer, as in the presence of God, such inquiries as these:

Do you find *divine love*, on the whole, advancing in your soul? Do you feel yourself more and more sensible of the presence of God; and does that sense grow more delightful to you than it formerly was? Can you, even when your natural spirits are weak and low, and you are not in any frame for the ardors and ecstasies of devotion, nevertheless find a pleasing rest, a calm repose of heart, in the thought that God is near you, and that he sees the secret sentiments of your soul, while you are, as it were, laboring up the hill, and casting a longing eye towards him, though you cannot say you enjoy any sensible communications from him? Is it agreeable to you to open your heart to his inspection and regard, to present it to him laid bare of every disguise, and to say, with David, "Thou, Lord, knowest thy servant?"[1] Do you find a growing esteem and approbation of that sacred law of God, which is the transcript of his moral perfections? Do you inwardly "esteem all his precepts concerning all things to be right?"[2] Do you discern, not only the necessity, but the reasonableness, the beauty, the pleasure of obedience; and feel a growing scorn and contempt of those things which may be offered as the price of your innocence, and would tempt you to sacrifice or hazard your interest in the divine favor and friendship? Do you find an ingenuous desire to please God, not only because he is so powerful, and has so many good and so many evil things entirely at his command, but from a veneration of his most amiable nature and character; and do you find your heart habitually reconciled to a most humble subjection both to his commanding and to his disposing will? Do you perceive that your own will is now more ready and disposed, in every circumstance, to bear the yoke, and to submit to the divine determination, whatever he appoints to be borne or forborne? Can you "in patience possess your soul?"[3] Can you maintain a more steady

1 2 Samuel 7:20.
2 Psalm 119:128.
3 Luke 21:19.

calmness and serenity, when God is striking at your dearest enjoyments in this world, and acting most directly contrary to your present interests, to your natural passions and desires? If you can, it is a most certain and noble sign that grace is growing up in you to a very vigorous state.

Examine, also, what affections you find in your heart *towards those who are about you, and towards the rest of mankind in general.* Do you find your heart overflow with undissembled and unrestrained benevolence? Are you more sensible than you once were, of those most endearing bonds which unite all men, and especially all Christians, into one community; which make them brethren and fellow-citizens? Do all the unfriendly passions die and wither in your soul, while the kind, social affections grow and strengthen? And though self-love was never the reigning passion since you became a true Christian, yet, as some remainders of it are still too ready to work inwardly, and to show themselves, especially as sudden occasions arise, do you perceive that you are getting the victory over them? Do you think of yourself only as one of a great number, whose particular interests and concerns are of little importance when compared with those of the community, and ought by all means, on all occasions, to be sacrificed to them?

Reflect especially on the temper of your mind towards those whom an unsanctified heart might be ready to imagine it had *some just excuse for excepting out of the list of those it loves,* and from whom you are ready to feel some secret alienation or aversion. How does your mind stand affected towards those who differ from you in their religious sentiments and practices? I do not say that Christian charity will require you to think every error harmless. It argues no want of love to a friend, in some cases, to fear lest his disorder should prove more fatal than he seems to imagine; no, sometimes the very tenderness of friendship may increase that apprehension. But to hate persons because we think they are mistaken, and to aggravate every difference in judgment or practice into a fatal and damnable error that destroys all Christian communion and love, is a symptom generally much worse than the evil it condemns. Do you love the image of Christ in a person who thinks himself obliged in conscience to profess and worship in a manner different from yourself? No, farther, can you love and honor that which is truly amiable and excellent in those in whom much is defective; in those in whom there is a mixture of bigotry and narrowness of spirit, which may lead them perhaps to slight, or even to censure you? Can you love them as the disciples and servants of Christ, who, through a mistaken zeal, may be ready to "cast out your name as evil,"[1] and to warn others against you as a dangerous person?

1 Luke 6:22.

This is none of the least triumphs of charity, nor any despicable evidence of an advance in religion.

And, on this head, reflect farther, how you can *bear injuries*. There is a certain hardness of soul in this respect, which argues a confirmed state in piety and virtue. Does every thing of this kind hurry and ruffle you, so as to put you on contrivances how you may recompense, or, at least, how you may disgrace and expose him who has done you the wrong? Or can you stand the shock calmly, and easily divert your mind to other objects, only, when you recollect these things, pitying and praying for those who, with the worst tempers and views, are assaulting you? This is a Christlike temper indeed, and he will own it as such; will own you as one of his soldiers, as one of his heroes: especially if it rises so far, as, instead of being "overcome of evil, to overcome evil with good."[1] Watch over your spirit and over your tongue, when injuries are offered, and see whether you be ready to meditate upon them, to aggravate them in your own view, to complain of them to others, and to lay on all the load of blame that you in justice can; or, whether you be ready to put the kindest construction upon the offense, to excuse it as far as reason will alloy, and where, after all, it will wear a black and odious aspect, to forgive it, heartily to forgive it, and that even before any submission is made or pardon asked; and in token of the

1 Romans 12:21.

sincerity of that forgiveness, to be contriving what can be done, by some benefit or other towards the injurious person, to teach him a better temper.

Examine farther, with regard to *other evils and calamities of life*, and even with regard to its uncertainties, how you can bear them. Do you find your soul is in this respect gathering strength? Have you fewer foreboding fears and disquieting alarms than you once had, as to what may happen in life? Can you trust the wisdom and goodness of God to order your affairs for you with more complacency and cheerfulness than formerly? Do you find yourself able to unite your thoughts more in surveying present circumstances, that you may collect immediate duty from them, though you know not what God will next appoint or call you to? And when you feel the smart of affliction, do you make a less matter of it? Can you transfer your heart more easily to heavenly and divine objects, without an anxious solicitude whether this or that burden be removed, if it may but be sanctified to promote your communion with God and your ripeness for glory?

Examine, also, whether you advance in *humility*. This is a silent, but most excellent grace; and they who are most eminent in it, are dearest to God, and most fit for the communications of his presence to them. Do you then feel your mind more emptied of proud and haughty imaginations, not prone so much to look back upon past services which it has performed, as forward to those which are yet before you, and inward upon the remaining imperfections of your heart? Do you more tenderly observe your daily failures and miscarriages, and find yourself disposed to mourn over those things before the Lord that once passed with you as slight matters, though, when you come to survey them as in the presence of God, you find they were not wholly involuntary or free from guilt? Do you feel in your breast a deeper apprehension of the infinite majesty of the blessed God, and of the glory of his natural and moral perfections, so as, in consequence of these views, to perceive yourself, as it were, annihilated in his presence, and to shrink into "less than nothing, and vanity?"[1] If this be your temper, God will look upon you with peculiar favor, and will visit you more and more with the distinguishing blessings of his grace.

But there is another great branch and effect of Christian humility, which it would be an unpardonable negligence to omit. Let me therefore farther inquire, are you more frequently renewing your application, your sincere, steady, determined *application to the righteousness and blood of Christ*, as being sensible how unworthy you are to appear before God otherwise than in him? And do the remaining corruptions of your heart humble you before him, though the disorders of your life are in a great measure cured? Are you more earnest to

1 Isaiah 40:17.

obtain the quickening influences of the Holy Spirit? And have you such a sense of your own weakness as to engage you to depend, in all the duties you perform, upon the communications of his grace "to help your infirmities?"[1] Can you, at the close of your most religious, exemplary, and useful days, blush before God for the deficiencies of them, while others perhaps may be ready to admire and extol your conduct? And while you give the glory of all that has been right to him from whom the strength and grace has been derived, are you coming to the blood of sprinkling, to free you from the guilt which mingles itself even with the best of your services? Do you learn to receive the bounties of Providence, not only with thankfulness as coming from God, but with a mixture of shame and confusion too, under a consciousness that you do not deserve them, and are continually forfeiting them? And do you justify Providence in your afflictions and disappointments, even while many are flourishing around you full in the bloom of prosperity, whose offenses have been more visible at least, and more notorious than yours?

Do you also advance in *zeal and activity for the service of God and the happiness of mankind?* Does your love show itself solid and sincere, by a continual flow of good works from it? Can you view the sorrows of others with tender compassion,

1 Romans 8:26.

and with projects and contrivances what you may do to relieve them? Do you feel in your breast that you are more frequently "devising liberal things,"[1] and ready to wave your own advantage or pleasure that you may accomplish them? Do you find your imagination teeming, as it were, with conceptions and schemes for the advancement of the cause and interest of Christ in the world, for the propagation of his Gospel, and for the happiness of your fellow-creatures? And do you not only pray, but act for it; act in such a manner as to show that you pray in earnest, and feel a readiness to do what little you can in this cause, even though others, who might, if they pleased, very conveniently do a vast deal more, will do nothing?

And, not to enlarge upon this copious subject, reflect once more, how your affections stand *with regard to this world and another.* Are you more deeply and practically convinced of the vanity of these "things which are seen, and are temporal?"[2] Do you perceive your expectations from them and your attachments to them to diminish? You are willing to stay in this world as long as your Father pleases; and it is right and well; but do you find your bonds so loosened from it, that you are willing, heartily willing, to leave it at the shortest warning; so that if God should see fit to summon you

1 Isaiah 32:8.
2 2 Corinthians 4:18.

away on a sudden, though it should be in the midst of your enjoyments, pursuits, expectations, and hopes, you would cordially consent to that remove, without saying, "Lord, let me stay a little while longer, to enjoy this or that agreeable entertainment, to finish this or that scheme?" Can you think, with an habitual calmness and hearty approbation, if such be the divine pleasure, of waking no more when you lie down on your bed, of returning home no more when you go out of your house? And yet, on the other hand, how great soever the burdens of life are, do you find a willingness to bear them, in submission to the will of your heavenly Father, though it should be to many future years, and though they should be years of far greater affliction than you have ever yet seen? Can you say calmly and steadily, if not with such overflowings of tender affection as you could desire, "Behold, 'thy servant,' thy child is 'in thine hand, do with me as seemeth good in thy sight?'[1] My will is melted into thine; to be lifted up or laid down, to be carried out or brought in, to be here or there, in this or that circumstance, just as thou pleasest, and as shall best suit thy great extensive plan, which it is impossible that I, or all the angels in heaven, should mend."

These, if I understand matters aright, are some of the most substantial evidences of growth and establishment in religion. Search after them: bless

1 2 Samuel 15:26.

God for them, so far as you discover them in yourself, and study to advance in them daily, under the influences of divine grace; to which I heartily recommend you, and to which I entreat you frequently to recommend yourself.

THE CHRISTIAN BREATHING EARNESTLY AFTER GROWTH IN GRACE

"O thou ever-blessed Fountain of natural and spiritual life! I thank thee that I live, and know the exercises and pleasures of a religious life. I bless thee that thou hast infused into me thine own vital breath, though I was once 'dead in trespasses and sins,'[1] so that I am become, in a sense peculiar to thine own children, 'a living soul.'[2] But it is my earnest desire that I may not only live but grow, 'grow in grace, and in the knowledge of my Lord and Saviour Jesus Christ.' May I be seeking after an increase of divine love to thee, my God and Father in Christ, of unreserved resignation to thy wise and holy will, and of extensive benevolence to my fellow-creatures! May I grow in patience and fortitude of soul, in humility and zeal, in spirituality and a heavenly disposition of mind, and in a concern 'that, whether present or absent, I may be

1 Ephesians 2:1.
2 Genesis 2:7.

accepted of the Lord,'[1] that whether I live or die, it may be for thy glory. In a word, as thou knows I hunger and thirst after righteousness, make me whatever thou would delight to see me! Draw on my soul, by the gentle influences of thy gracious Spirit, every trace and every feature which thine eye, heavenly Father, may survey with pleasure, and which thou may acknowledge as thine own image. This I ask and hope through our Lord and Saviour Jesus Christ: to him be glory both now and for ever."

---

1 2 Corinthians 5:9.

The Well-Spent Day

by Rev. Philip Doddridge, D.D.

MY DEAR FRIEND—Since you desire my thoughts in writing, and at large, on the subject of our late conversation, namely, *by what particular methods in our daily conduct a life of devotion and usefulness may be most happily maintained and secured*, I set myself with cheerfulness to recollect and digest the hints which I then gave you; hoping that it may be of some service to you in your most important interests, and may also fix on my own mind a deeper sense of obligation to govern my own life by the rules I offer to others. I esteem attempts of this kind among the pleasantest fruits and the surest cements of friendship; and, as I hope ours will last for ever, I am persuaded a mutual care to cherish sentiments of this kind will add everlasting endearments to it.

The directions you will expect from me on this occasion, naturally divide themselves into three heads: How we are to regard God, *in the beginning, the progress, and the close of the day.*

I. In the *beginning of the day,* it should certainly be our care to lift up our hearts to God, as soon as we awake, and while we are arising; and then to set ourselves seriously and immediately to the secret devotion of the morning.

The first of these seems exceedingly natural. There are so many things that may suggest a great variety of pious reflections and ejaculations, which are so obvious, that one would think a serious mind could hardly miss them. The ease and cheerfulness of our minds at our first awaking; the refreshment we find from sleep; the security we have enjoyed in that defenseless state; the provision of warm and decent apparel; the cheerful light of the returning sun; or even—what is not unfit to mention to you—the contrivances of art, taught and furnished by the great Author of all our conveniences, to supply us with many useful hours of life in the absence of the sun; the hope of returning to the dear society of our friends; the prospect of spending another day in the service of God, and the improvement of our own minds; and, above all, the lively hope of a joyful resurrection to an eternal day of happiness and glory: any of these particulars, and many more which I do not mention, may furnish us with matter of pleasing reflection and cheerful praise, while we are rising. And, for our further assistance, when we are alone at this time, it may not be improper to speak sometimes to ourselves, and sometimes to our heavenly Father, in the natural expressions of joy and thankfulness. Permit me, sir, to add, that if we find our hearts in such a frame at our first awaking, even *that* is just matter of praise, and the rather, as perhaps it is an answer to the prayer with which we lay down.

For the exercise of secret devotion in a morning, which I hope will generally be our first work after we rise, I cannot prescribe an exact method to another. You must, my dear friend, consult your own taste in some measure. The constituent parts of the service are, in general, plain. Were I to propose a particular model for those who have half or three quarters of an hour at command, it should be this:

To begin the stated devotions of the day with a solemn act of praise, acknowledging the mercies we had been reflecting on while rising: never forgetting to mention Christ, as the great foundation of all our enjoyments, and all our hopes, or to return thanks for the influences of the blessed Spirit, which have led our hearts to God, or are then engaging us to seek him. This, as well as other offices of devotion, afterwards mentioned, must be performed attentively and sincerely; for not to offer our praises heartily, is, in the sight of God, not to praise at all. We may properly conclude this address with an explicit renewal of our covenant with God, declaring our continued resolution of being devoted to him, and particularly of living to his glory the ensuing day.

It may then be suitable to take a prospect of the day before us, so far as we can probably foresee, in the general, where, and how it may be spent; and seriously to reflect, "How shall I employ myself for God this day? What business is to be done, and in what order? What opportunities may I expect, either of doing or receiving good? What temptations am I likely to be assaulted with, in any place, company, or circumstances, to which I may be introduced? In what instances have I lately failed? And how shall I be safest now?"

After this review, it will be proper to offer up a short prayer, begging that God would quicken us to each of these foreseen duties; that he would fortify us against each of these apprehended dangers; that he would grant us success in such or such a business undertaken for his glory; and, also, that he would help us to discover and improve unforeseen opportunities, to resist unexpected temptations, and to bear patiently any affliction which may surprise us in the day on which we are entering.

I would advise you, after this, to read some portion of Scripture, particularly from those parts of the Bible which are of a more devotional and practical kind. Here, take such instructions as readily present themselves to your thoughts; repeat them over to your own conscience, and charge your heart religiously to observe them, and act upon them, under a sense of the divine authority which attends them. And if you pray over this part of revelation with your Bible open before you, it may impress your memory and your heart yet more deeply, and may form you to a copiousness and variety, both of thought and expression, in prayer.

It might be proper to close these devotions with a Psalm or Hymn: and I rejoice with you, that through the pious care of Dr. Watts, and some other sacred poets, we are provided with so rich a variety, for the assistance of the closet and family on these occasions, as well as for the service of the sanctuary.

II. The most material directions which have occurred to me, relating to the *progress of the day*, are these: That we be serious in devotion; that we be diligent in business; that we be temperate, and prudent in recreations; that we carefully remark providences; that we cautiously guard against temptations; that we keep up a lively and humble dependence upon the divine influence, suitable to every emergency; that we govern our thoughts well in solitude, and our discourse well in conversation.

1. For *seriousness in devotion*, whether public or domestic, let us take a few moments, before we enter upon such solemnities, to pause, and reflect on the perfections of the God we are addressing, on the importance of the business we are coming

about, on the pleasure and advantage of a regular and devout attendance, and on the guilt and folly of a hypocritical formality. When engaged, let us maintain a strict watchfulness over our own spirits, and check the first wanderings of thought. And, when the duty is over, let us immediately look back on the manner in which it has been performed, and ask our own consciences whether we have reason to conclude that we are accepted of God in it. For there is a certain manner of going through these offices, which our hearts will immediately tell us it is impossible for God to approve. And, if we have inadvertently fallen into it, we ought to be deeply humbled before God for it, lest our prayers become sin.[1]

2. As for the *hours of worldly business*, whether it be that of the hands, or whether it be the labor of a learned life, let us attend to the prosecution of it with a sense of God's authority, and with a regard to his glory. Let us avoid a dreaming, sluggish, indolent temper, which nods over its work, and does only the business of one hour in two or three. In opposition to this, which runs through the life of some people, who yet think they are never idle, let us endeavor to despatch as much as we well can in a little time; considering that it is but a little we have in all. And let us be habitually sensible of the need we have of the divine blessing, to make our labors successful.

3. For *seasons of diversion*, let us take care that

1 Psalm 109:7.

our recreations be well chosen; that they be pursued with a good intention, to fit us for a renewed application to the labors of life; and then that they be used only in subordination to the honor of God, the great end of all our actions. Let us take heed that our hearts be not estranged from God by them, and that they do not take up too much of our time: always remembering, that the faculties of human nature, and the advantages of the Christian revelation, were not given us in vain; but that we are always to be in pursuit of some great and honorable end, and to indulge ourselves in amusements and diversions no further than as they make a part in a scheme of rational and manly, benevolent and pious conduct.

4. For the *observation of providences*, it will be useful to regard the divine interposition, in our comforts and in our afflictions.

In our comforts, whether more common or extraordinary: that we find ourselves in continual health; that we are furnished with food for support and pleasure; that we have so many friends, and those so good and so happy; that our business goes on prosperously; that we go out, and come in, safely; and that we enjoy composure and cheerfulness of spirit, without which nothing else can be enjoyed. All these should be regarded as providential favors, and due acknowledgments should be made to God on these accounts, as we pass through such agreeable scenes.

On the other hand, Providence is to be regarded in every disappointment, in every loss, in every pain, in every instance of unkindness from those who have professed friendship. And we should endeavor to argue ourselves into a patient submission, from the consideration that the hand of God is always mediately, if not immediately, in each of them; and that if they are not properly the work of Providence, they are at least under its direction. It is a reflection which we should particularly make with relation to those little cross accidents, (as we are ready to call them) and those infirmities and follies in the temper and conduct of our intimate friends, which else may be ready to discompose us. And it is the more necessary to guard our minds here, as wise and good men often lose the command of themselves on these comparatively little occasions; who, calling up reason and religion to their assistance, stand the shock of great calamities with fortitude and resolution.

5. For *watchfulness against temptations*, it is necessary, when changing our place or our employment, to reflect, "What snares attend me here?" And as this should be our habitual care, so we should especially guard against those snares which in the morning we foresaw. And when we are entering on those circumstances in which we expected the assault, we should reflect, especially if it be a matter of great importance, "Now the combat is

going to begin; now God and the blessed angels are observing what constancy, what fortitude there are in my soul; and how far the divine authority, and the remembrance of my own prayers and resolutions, will weigh with me when it comes to a trial."

6. As for *dependence on divine grace* for influence, it must be universal; and since we always need it, we must never forget that necessity. A moment spent in humble, fervent breathings after the communications of the divine assistance, will do more good than many minutes spent in mere reasonings. And though indeed these should not be neglected, since the light of reason is a kind of divine illumination, yet still it ought to be pursued in a due sense of our dependence on the Father of lights, or where we think ourselves wisest, we may become vain in our imaginations.[1]

Let us therefore always call upon God; and say, for instance, when we are going to pray, "Lord, fix my attention, awaken my holy affections, and pour out upon me the spirit of grace and of supplication!"[2] When taking up the Bible, or any other good book, "Open thou mine eyes, that I may behold wondrous things out of thy law![3] Enlighten mine understanding, warm my heart. May my good resolutions be confirmed, and all the course of my life be in a proper

---

1 Romans 1:21, 22.
2 Zechariah 12:10.
3 Psalm 119:18.

manner regulated." When addressing ourselves to any worldly business, "Lord, prosper thou the work of mine hands upon me,[1] and give thy blessing to my honest endeavors." When going to any kind of recreation, "Lord, bless my refreshments. Let me not forget thee in them, but still keep thy glory in view." When coming into company, "Lord, may I *do*, and *get* good. Let no corrupt communications proceed out of my mouth, but that which is good to the use of edifying, that it may minister grace to the hearers."[2] When entering upon difficulties, "Lord, give me that wisdom which is profitable to direct."[3] "Teach me thy way, and lead me in a plain path."[4] When encountering temptations, "Let thy strength, O gracious Redeemer, be made perfect in my weakness."[5] These instances may illustrate the design of this direction, though they are far from a complete enumeration of all the circumstances in which it is to be regarded.

7. For the *government of our thoughts* in solitude, let us accustom ourselves, on all occasions, to exercise a due command over our thoughts. Let us take care of those entanglements of passion, and those attachments to any present interest and view,

---

1 Psalm 90:17.
2 Ephesians 4:29.
3 Ecclesiastes 10:10.
4 Psalm 27:11.
5 2 Corinthians 12:9.

which would deprive us of our power over them. Let us set before us some profitable subject of thought, such as the perfections of the blessed God, the love of Christ, the value of time, the certainty and importance of death and judgment, and the eternity of happiness or misery which is to follow. Let us also, at such intervals, reflect on what we have observed as to the state of our own souls, with regard to the advance or decline of religion; or on the last sermon we have heard, or the last portion of Scripture we have read. It may be very useful to select some one verse of Scripture, which we had met with in the morning, and to treasure it up in our mind, resolving to think of that at any time when we are at a loss for matter of pious reflection.

8. Lastly, for the *government of our discourse* in company, we should take great care that nothing may escape us, which can expose us or our Christian profession to censure and reproach; nothing injurious to those that are absent, or to those that are present; nothing malignant or insincere; nothing which may corrupt; nothing which may provoke or mislead those about us. Nor should we, by any means, be content that what we say is innocent; it should be our desire that it may be edifying to ourselves and others. In this view, we should endeavor to have some subject of useful discourse always ready; in which we may be assisted by the hints given about furniture for thought, under the

former head. We should watch for proper opportunities of introducing useful reflections; and if a
pious friend attempt to do it, we should endeavor
to second him immediately. When the conversation does not turn directly on religious subjects, we
should endeavor to make it improving some other
way. And in the pauses of discourse, it may not
be improper to lift up a holy ejaculation to God,
that his grace may assist us and our friends in our
endeavors to do good to each other; that all we say
and do may be worthy the character of reasonable
creatures, and of Christians.

III. The directions for a religious *closing of the
day*, which I shall here mention, are only two: Let
us see to it, that the secret duties of the evening be
well performed; and lie down on our bed in a pious
frame.

1. For *secret devotion in the evening*, I would
propose a method something different from that in
the morning; but still, as then, with due allowance
for circumstances, which may make unthought of
alterations proper, I should advise you to read a
portion of Scripture, in the first place, with suitable reflections; then, to read a Hymn or Psalm:
after this, to enter on self-examination, to be fol-
lowed by a prayer to be formed on this review of
the day. In this address to the throne of grace, it will
be highly proper to entreat that God would pardon
the omissions and offenses of the day; to praise him

for mercies temporal and spiritual; to recommend ourselves to his protection for the ensuing night; with proper petitions for others, whom we ought to bear on our hearts before him; and particularly for those friends with whom we have conversed or corresponded in the preceding day.

Before I quit this head, I must take the liberty to remind you, that self-examination is so important a duty, that it would be worth our while to spend a few words upon it. And this branch of it is so easy, that when we have proper questions before us, any person of a common understanding may hope to go through it with advantage, under the divine blessing. I offer you, therefore, the following queries, which I hope you will, with such alterations as you think requisite, keep near you for daily use.

"Did I awake as with God this morning, and rise with a grateful sense of his goodness? How were the secret devotions of the morning performed? Did I offer my solemn praises, and renew the dedication of myself to God, with becoming attention and suitable affections? Did I lay my scheme for the business of the day wisely and well? How did I read the Scriptures? Did it do my heart good, or was it a mere amusement? How have the other stated devotions of the day been attended, whether in the family or in public? Have I pursued the common business of the day with diligence and spirituality; doing every thing in season, and with all convenient dispatch, and as unto the Lord?[1] What time have I lost this day, in the morning, or the forenoon, in the afternoon, or the evening; and what has occasioned the loss of it? With what temper, and under what regulations, have the recreations of this day been pursued? Have I seen the hand of God in my mercies, health, cheerfulness, food, clothing, books, preservation in journeys, success of business, conversation, and kindness of friends? Have I seen it in afflictions, and particularly in little things which have a tendency to vex and disquiet me? Have I received my comforts thankfully, and my afflictions submissively? How have I guarded against the temptations of the day, particularly against this or that temptation which I foresaw in the morning? Have I maintained a humble dependence on divine influences? Have I lived by faith in the Son of God,[2] and regarded Christ this day as my Teacher and Governor, my Atonement and Intercessor, my Example and Guardian, my Strength and Forerunner? Have I been looking forward to death and eternity this day, and considered myself as a probationer for heaven, and, through grace, an expectant of it? Have I governed my thoughts well, especially in such or such an interval of solitude? How was my subject of thought this day chosen, and how was it regarded? Have I governed

1 Colossians 3:23.
2 Galatians 2:20.

THE WELL SPENT DAY

my discourses well in such or such company? Did I say nothing passionate, mischievous, slanderous, imprudent, impertinent? Has my heart this day been full of love to God, and to all mankind; and have I sought, and found, and improved, opportunities of doing and getting good? With what attention and improvement have I read the Scripture this evening? How was self-examination performed the last night; and how have I profited this day by any remarks I then made on former negligence and mistakes? With what temper did I then lie down, and compose myself?"

2. I conclude with noticing the sentiments with which we should *compose ourselves to sleep*. It becomes us to think of the divine goodness, in adding another day, and the mercies of it, to the former days and mercies of our life; to take notice of the indulgence of Providence, in giving us commodious habitations and easy beds, and continuing to us such health of body, that we can lay ourselves down at ease upon them, and such serenity of mind as leaves us any room to hope for refreshing sleep—a refreshment, to be sought, not merely as an indulgence to animal nature, but as what our wise Creator, in order to keep us humble in the midst of so many infirmities, has been pleased to make necessary to our being able to renew his service with renewed alacrity. Thus may our sleeping, as well as our waking hours, be in some sense

devoted to God. And when we are just going to resign ourselves to the image of death—to what one of the ancients beautifully calls *its lesser mysteries*—it is also evidently proper to think seriously of that end of all the living, and to renew those actings of repentance and faith which we should judge necessary, if we were to wake no more here.

HOW TO MAKE THE MOST OF A DAY

1. Rise early, and begin it with God. Time waits upon each of us when we awake, and says, What wilt thou have me do today? Our answer to this inquiry is of no trivial importance.

2. We must have a plan, general and subordinate. Our great moralist, Johnson, remarks, "I believe it is best to throw life into a method, that every hour may bring its employment, and every employment have its hour. If every thing be kept in a certain place, when any thing is worn out or consumed, the vacuity which it leaves will show what is wanting; so, if every part of time has its appropriate duty, the hour will call into remembrance its engagement."

3. We must undertake no more than we can reasonably expect to perform, and do one thing at a time.

4. While we should avoid voluntary hindrances, if interruptions occur, instead of wasting our time

in fruitless regret, we should endeavor to improve passing circumstances.

5. We must carefully gather up fragments. "Betwixt the more earnest employments and important occurrences of life there are several intervals, which, though in one day they may be inconsiderable, yet in the whole time of a man's life they amount to a great deal of it. These uncertain intervals are often lost; either as not valued by most people, or neglected, though not despised, by good men, for want of skill to make use of them. As goldsmiths and refiners preserve the very sweepings of their shop, to save the filings of gold and silver, so a Christian ought to be very careful of those small portions of time which are more precious than metals."

6. We should aim at strict punctuality in engagements. A man who wants punctuality, not only wastes his own time, but often intrudes upon that of others, which may be still more valuable.

7. We must guard against a spirit of procrastination. The sacrifices under the Law were offered "as the duty of every day required";[1] "whatsoever thy hand findeth to do, do it with thy might."[2] We must also be watchful over ourselves, lest a habit of unprofitable anxiety, as to the future, rob us of our time. Many hours are consumed in wild and

---

1 2 Chronicles 8:13.
2 Ecclesiastes 9:10.

groundless anticipations of evil.

8. To recall at night the transactions of the day, and endeavor to make the following a practical comment on the past, would be highly advantageous. To inquire, What has the day done for me? Has it set me nearer heaven? Has it brought an increase of knowledge and virtue? Has it been devoted to the service of God and man? Or, has it been spent in sloth, sensuality, or self-pleasing?

9. Should our active powers be suspended, and a season of languor and sickness intervene, there are still duties to be performed. Days of affliction are not *idle days*. "They who *sow* in tears shall reap in joy."[1] He who goes forth weeping, bearing "the precious seed" of faith, patience, prayer, submission, penitence, and hope, shall doubtless come again rejoicing, bringing his sheaves with him; and all who have diligently improved the talents committed to them, shall serve God when *"time shall be no longer,"*[2] without imperfection, without weariness, and without end.

---

1 Psalm 126:5.
2 Revelation 10:6.

Family Worship

by Rev. Philip Doddridge, D.D.

This address may come into the hands of many who have long been exemplary for their diligence and zeal in the duties I am about to recommend. Such, I hope, will be confirmed, by what they read, in pursuing the good resolutions they have taken, and the good customs they have formed; and will also be excited more earnestly to endeavor to contribute towards introducing the like into other families over which they have any influence, and especially into those which may branch out from their own by the settlement of children and servants.

But I have those principally in view who have hitherto lived in the omission of family prayer.

While I write this I have that awakening Scripture before me: "Pour out thy fury upon the heathen that know thee not, and upon *the families that call not upon thy name.*"[1] I appeal to you

1 Jeremiah 10:25.

whether this does not strongly imply that every family which is not a *heathen family*, which is not quite ignorant of the living and true God, will call upon his name. Well may it then pain my heart, to think that there should be a professedly *Christian family* whom this dreadful character suits; well may it pain my heart, to think of the divine fury which may be poured out on the heads and on the members of it; and well may it make me desirous to do my utmost to secure you and yours from every appearance and possibility of such danger. Excuse the earnestness with which I may address you. I really fear, lest, while you delay, the fire of the divine displeasure should fall upon you.[1] And as I adore the patience of God in having thus long suspended the storm, I am anxious about every hour's delay, lest it should fall heavier.

What I desire and entreat of you is, that you would honor and acknowledge God in your families, by calling them together, every day, to hear some part of his Word read to them, and to join, for a few minutes at least, in your confessions, prayers, and praises to him. And is this a cause that should need to be pleaded at large by a great variety of united motives? Truly the petition seems so reasonable, and a compliance with it, from one who has not quite renounced religion, might seem so natural, that one would think the bare proposing of

1 Genesis 19:16, 17.

it would suffice. Yet experience tells us, it is much otherwise. Some, who maintain a public profession of religion, have refused, and will continue to refuse, year after year.

Reflect, sir, (for I address myself to every particular person) seriously reflect on the *reasonableness* of family religion. Must not your conscience presently tell you, it is fit that persons who receive so many mercies together, should acknowledge them together? Can you in your mind be satisfied, that you and your nearest relatives should pay no joint homage to that God who has set you in your family, and who has given to you, and to the several members of it, so many domestic enjoyments? Can it be right, if you have any sense of these things, each of you in your own hearts, that the sense of them should be concealed and smothered there, and that you should never join in your grateful acknowledgments to him? Can you imagine it reasonable, that when you have a constant dependence upon him for so many mercies, without the recurrence of which your family would be a scene of misery, you should never present yourselves together in his presence to ask them at his hand? Upon what principle is *public* worship to be recommended and urged, if not by such as have their proportionable weight here?

Indeed, the force of these considerations has not only been known and acknowledged by the people of God in all ages; we have not only Noah and

Abraham, Joshua and David, Job and Daniel, each under a much darker dispensation than ours, as examples of it; but even the poor heathen had their household images, some of them in private chapels, and others about the common hearth, where the family used to worship them by frequent prayers and sacrifices. And the brass, and wood, and stone, of which they consisted, shall, as it were, cry out against you—shall rise up against you and condemn you, if, while you call yourselves the worshippers of the one living and eternal God, and boast in the revelation you have received by his prophets and by his Son, you presume to omit a homage which the stupid worshippers of such vanities as these failed not to present to them, while they called them their gods. Be persuaded then, I beseech you, to be consistent in your conduct. Either give up all pretences to religion, or maintain a steady and uniform regard to it, at home as well as abroad, in the family as well as in the closet or at church.

1. Consider the happy influence which the duty I am recommending might have upon the young members of your family, the *children* and *servants* committed to your care. For I now consider you as a parent and a master. *The father of a family* is a phrase that comprehends both these relations, and with great propriety, as humanity obliges us to endeavor to take a parental care of all under our roof. And indeed you ought to consider your servants, in

this view, with a tender regard. They are probably in the flower of life, for that is the age which is commonly spent in service; and you should recollect how possible it is, that this may be, if rightly improved, the best opportunity their whole life may afford them, for learning religion, and being brought under the power of it. Let them not, if they should finally perish, have cause to testify before God in the day of their condemnation, that under your roof they learned the neglect and forgetfulness of God, and all that their pious parents, perhaps in a much inferior station of life to you, had in earlier days been attempting to teach them. Or, if they come to you quite ignorant of religion, as, if they come from prayerless families, it is very probable that they do, have compassion upon them, I entreat you, and endeavor to give them those advantages which they never yet had, and which it is too probable, as things are generally managed, they never will have, if you will not afford them.

But I would especially, if I might be allowed to borrow the pathetic words of Job, *entreat you by the children of your own body.*[1] I would now, as it were, present them all before you, and beseech you by the bowels of parental affection, that to all the other tokens of tenderness and love, you would not refuse to add this, without which many of the rest may be worse than in vain.

1 Job 19:17.

Give me leave to plead with you, as the instruments of introducing them into being. O remember, it is indeed a debased and corrupted nature that you have conveyed to them. Consider, that the world, into which you have been the means of bringing them, is a place in which they are surrounded by many temptations, and in which, as they advance in life, they must expect many more; so that it is much to be feared, that they will remain ignorant and forgetful of God, if they do not learn from you to love and serve him. For how can it be expected that they should learn this at all, if you give them no advantages for receiving and practising the lesson at home?

And let me further urge and entreat you to remember, that these dear children are committed to your special care by God their Creator, who has made them thus dependent upon you, that you might have an opportunity of forming their minds, and of influencing them to a right temper and conduct. And can this by any means be effectually done, if you do not at proper times call them together to attend to the instructions of the Word of God, and to join in solemn prayers and supplications to him? At least, is it possible that it should be done any other way with equal advantage, if this be not added to the rest?

Family worship is a most proper way of teaching children religion, as you teach them language by insensible degrees—a little one day, and a little another; for to them *line must be upon line, and precept upon precept.* They may learn to conceive aright of the divine perfections, when they hear you daily acknowledging and adoring them; their hearts may be early touched with remorse for sin, when they hear your confessions poured out before God; they will know what mercies they are to ask for themselves, by observing what turn your petitions take; your intercessions may diffuse into their minds a spirit of love to mankind, a concern for the interest of the church and of their country; and your solemn thanksgivings for the bounties of Providence, and for benefits of a spiritual nature, may affect their hearts with those impressions towards the gracious Author of all, which may excite in their little breasts love to him, the most noble and genuine principle of all true and acceptable religion. Thus they may embrace Christ in their earliest years, and grow in the knowledge and love of truth as they do in stature. Indeed, were this duty properly attended to, it might be expected that all Christian families would, according to their respective sizes and circumstances, become nurseries of piety; and you would see, in the most convincing view, the wisdom of Providence, in making human infants so much more dependent on their parents, and so much more incapable of shifting for themselves, than the offspring of inferior creatures are.

Let me then entreat you, my dear friends, to look on your children the very next time you see them, and ask your own heart, how can you answer it to God and to them, that you deprive them of such advantages as these—advantages without which it is to be feared your care of them in other respects will turn to but little account, should they be ever so prosperous in life. For what is prosperity in life, without the knowledge, and fear, and love of God? What but the poison of the soul, which swells and kills it? What but the means of making it more certainly, more deeply, more intolerably miserable? In short, not to mention the happy influence which family devotion may have on their temporal affairs, by drawing down the divine blessing, and by forming their minds to those virtues which pave the way to wealth and reputation, health and contentment, which make no enemies, and attract many friends; it is, with respect to the eternal world, the greatest cruelty to your children to neglect giving them those advantages which no other attentions in education, exclusive of these, can afford; and it is impossible that you should ever be able to give them any other equivalent. If you do your duty in this respect, they will have reason to bless you, living and dying; and if you neglect it, take care that you and they come not, in consequence of that neglect, into a world where (horrid as the thought may seem) you will be for ever cursing each other!

2. Let me now press you to consider how much *your own interest* is concerned in the matter.

Your *spiritual* interest is concerned. Let me seriously ask you, do you not need those advantages for religion, which the performance of family duty will give you, added to those of a more secret and a more public nature, if peradventure *they* are regarded by you? These instructions, these adorations, these confessions, these supplications, these intercessions, these thanksgivings, which may be so useful to your children and servants—may they not be useful to yourself? May not your own heart have some peculiar advantage for being impressed, when you are the mouth of others in these domestic devotions, beyond what, in a private station of life, it is otherwise possible that you should have? No, the remoter influence they may have on your conduct, in other respects, and at other times, when considered merely in the general, as religious exercises performed by you in your family, is to be recollected as an argument of vast importance.

A sense of common decency would engage you, if you pray with your family, to avoid a great many evils, which would appear doubly evil in a father or a master who kept up such religious exercises in his house. Do you imagine that, if reading the Scriptures, and family prayer, were introduced into the houses of some of your neighbors—drunkenness, and lewdness, and cursing, and swearing, and profaning the Lord's Day, would not, like so many evil demons, be quickly driven out? The master of a family would not, for shame, indulge them, if he kept up nothing more than the form of duty; and his reformation, though only external, and at first on a kind of constraint, would carry with it the reformation of many more, who have such a dependence on his favor as they would not sacrifice, though, by a madness very prevalent among the children of men, they can venture to sacrifice their souls to every trifle.

And may it not perhaps be your more immediate concern, to recollect, that if you prayed with your family, you would yourself be more careful to "abstain from all appearance of evil?"[1] You would find out a way to suppress that turbulency of passion which may now be ready to break out before you are aware, and other imprudences, in which your own heart would check you by saying, "Does this become one that is by and by to kneel down with his children and servants, and adore God with them, and pray against everything which displeases God, and makes us unfit for the heavenly world?" I will not say this will cure everything that is wrong, but I believe you are already persuaded, it would often have a very good influence. And I fear it is the secret desire of indulging some irregularities without such a restraint, that, shameful as such a

1 1 Thessalonians 5:22.

conduct is, has driven out family prayer from several houses, and has prevented its introduction into others. But if you have any secret disinclination of heart against it, in this view, it becomes you to be most seriously alarmed for your spiritual condition.

After this it may seem a matter of small importance to urge the good influence which a proper discharge of family duty may have upon your own *temporal affairs*, both by restraining you from many evils, and engaging you to a proper conduct yourself, and also by impressing your children and servants with a sense of religion. And it is certain, the more careful they are of their duty to God, the more likely they will be to perform their duty to you. Nor can anything strengthen your natural authority among them more, than your presiding in such solemnities, if supported by a suitable conduct. But I would hope nobler motives will have a superior weight. And therefore, waving this topic, I entreat you, as the last argument, to consider,

3. The influence it may have on a *general reformation*, and on the *propagation of religion* to those who are yet unborn. You ought to consider every child and servant in your family, as one who may be a source, not only of life, but, in some degree, of character and happiness to those who are hereafter to rise into being; yes, whose conduct may in part affect those that are to descend from them in a remote generation. If they grow up, while under

your eye, ignorant of religion, they will certainly be much less capable of teaching it to others; for these are the years of discipline, and, if they are neglected now, there is little probability of their receiving instruction afterwards. Nor is this all the evil consequence; for it is highly probable, that they will think themselves sanctioned by your example in a like negligence, and so you may entail *heathenism,* under the name of Christianity, on your descendants and theirs for ages to come. Whereas your diligence and zeal might be remembered and imitated by them, perhaps when you are in your grave; and the stock, which they first received from you, might with rich improvements be communicated to great numbers, so that *one generation after another* might learn to fear and serve the Lord. On the whole, God only knows what a church may arise from one godly family; what a harvest may spring up from a single seed; and on the other hand, it is impossible to say how many souls may at length perish by the treacherous neglect of a single person, and, to speak plainly, by your own.

These, sir, are the arguments I have to plead with you, and which I have selected out of many more. And now give me leave seriously to ask you, as in the presence of God, whether there be not on the whole an unanswerable force in them? And if there is, what follows but that you immediately yield to that force, and set up family worship *this very day?* For, I think, I hardly would thank you for a resolution to do it *tomorrow;* so little do I expect from that resolution. How can you excuse yourself in the continued omission? Bring the matter before God. He will be the final judge of it; and if you cannot debate the question as in his presence, it is the sign of a bad cause, and of a bad heart too, which is conscious of the badness of the cause; and yet will not give it up, nor comply with a duty, of your obligation to which you are secretly convinced, while in effect you say, "I will go on in this sin, and venture the consequence." O! it is a dreadful venture, and will be found *provoking the Lord to jealousy, as if you were stronger than he.*[1]

God is represented as giving this reason to his angels for a particular favor to be bestowed on Abraham. "I know that he will command his children and household to keep the way of the Lord, that he may obtain the blessing promised."[2] Did he not hereby intend to declare his approbation of the care which Abraham took to support religion in his family? And can it be supported in a total neglect of prayer?

Again: Do you not, in your conscience, think that the Spirit of God meant that we should take Joshua for an example, when he tells us, that he resolved, and publicly declared the resolution, *that*

1 1 Corinthians 10:22.
2 Genesis 18:19.

he and his house would serve the Lord;[1] which must express a religious care of his family too?

Do you not believe, that the blessed Spirit meant it as a commendation of Job, that he *offered sacrifices for all his children,*[2]—sacrifices undoubtedly attended with prayers—when he feared lest the gayety of their hearts, in their successive feastings, might have betrayed them into some moral evil?

And was it not to do an honor to David, that the Scripture informs us that "he went home to bless his household";[3] that is, to perform some solemn act of domestic worship, when he had been spending the whole day in public devotion?

And do you think, when our blessed Lord, whose life was employed in religious services, so frequently took his disciples apart to pray with them, that he did not intend this as an example to us, of praying with those under our special care, or in other words, with the members of our own family, who are most immediately so? Or can you, by any imaginable artifice, delude yourself so far as to think, that when we are solemnly charged and commanded to pray "with all prayer and supplication,"[4] this kind of prayer is not included in that apostolical injunction?

---

1 Joshua 24:15.
2 Job 1:5.
3 2 Samuel 6:20.
4 Ephesians 6:18.

Were there not one praying family in the whole
world, I think it should instigate you to the practice, rather than tempt you to neglect it, and you
should press on, as ambitious of the glory of lead-
ing the way. For what could be a nobler object of
ambition, than to be pointed out by the blessed
God himself, as Job was; of whom he said, with a
kind of triumph, "Hast thou considered my servant
Job, that there is none like him in the land, or even
on the earth?"[1] But blessed be God, the neglect
we have supposed is far from being universal. Let
it however rejoice us, if God may say, "There are
such and such families, distinguishable from those
in their neighborhood on this account; as prevalent
as the neglect of family prayer is, *they* have the resolution to practice it, and, like my servant Daniel,
fear not the reproach and contempt which profane
and ungodly men may cast upon them, if they may
but honor me and engage my favor: I know them;
I hearken and hear, and a book of remembrance is
written before me for them that fear me, and think
on my name."

Say not you have no *time*. How many hours
in a week do you spend for amusement, while you
have none for devotion in your family? And do you
indeed hold the blessing of God so very cheap, and
think it a matter of so little importance, that you
conclude your business must succeed the worse, if

1 Job 1:8.

a few minutes were daily taken to implore it before
your family? Let me rather admonish you, that the
greater your business is, the more need you have to
pray earnestly that your heart may not be engrossed
by it. And I would beg leave further to remind you,
that if your hurry of business were indeed so great as
the objection supposes, (which I believe is seldom
the case) prudence alone might suggest that you
should endeavor to contract it. For there are certain boundaries beyond which a wise and faithful
care cannot extend; and as an attempt to go beyond
these boundaries has generally its foundation in
avarice, so it often has its end in poverty and ruin.
But if you were ever so secure of succeeding for this
world, how dear might you and your children pay
for that success, if all the blessed consequences of
family religion, for time and for eternity, were to
be given up as the price of that very small part of
your gains, which is owing to the minutes you take
from these exercises, that you may give them to the
world? For you plainly perceive the question is only
about them, and by no means about a strenuous
application to the proper duties of your secular calling through the day. And if you will be rich upon
such profane terms as are here supposed, (for truly
I can call them no better than profane) you will
probably plunge yourself into final perdition, and
may in the mean time "pierce yourself through with
many sorrows"; while religious families will learn,

by happy experience, that the blessing of the Lord, which they are so often imploring together, "maketh rich, and he addeth no sorrow with it,"[1] or that "a little, with the fear of the Lord, is better than great treasures," with that intermingled trouble,[2] which in the neglect of God must necessarily be expected.

As for *ability*, where the heart is rightly disposed, it does not require any *uncommon abilities* to discharge family worship in a decent and edifying manner. "The heart of the wise," in this respect, "teacheth his mouth, and addeth knowledge to his lips,"[3] and "out of the fullness of it," when it is indeed full of pious affections, "the mouth will naturally speak."[4] Plain, short sentences, uttered just as they rise in the mind, will be best understood by them that join with you; and they will be more pleasing to God than anything which should proceed from ostentation and parade.

I must also desire you to consider, how many helps you may easily procure. The Scripture is a large and noble magazine of the most proper sentiments, and most expressive language, which, if you will attend to it with a becoming regard, will soon furnish you for this good work. We have too in our language a great variety of excellent forms of prayer

1 Proverbs 10:22.
2 Proverbs 15:16.
3 Proverbs 16:23.
4 Luke 6:45.

for families as well as for private persons, which you may use, at least at first, with great profit. And if it is too laborious to you to learn them by heart, or if, having learned them, you dare not trust your memory, what should forbid your reading them reverently and devoutly? I hope the main thing is, that God be reverently and sincerely adored; that suitable blessings, temporal and spiritual, be sought from him for ourselves and others; and cordial thanksgivings returned to him for the various gifts of his continual bounty.

If *opposition* be made in your family, you ought to let any in whom you discover it know that your measures are fixed, and that you cannot and will not resign that just authority which the laws of God and man give you in your own house, to their unhappy temper, or daring impiety.

May God give you resolution immediately to make the attempt! And may he assist and accept you, and scatter down every desirable blessing of Providence and of grace on you and yours! So that this day may become memorable in your lives, as a season from which you may date a prosperity and a joy hitherto unknown, how happy soever you may have been in former years; for very imperfect, I am sure, must that domestic happiness be, in which domestic religion has no part.

But if, after all, you will not be persuaded, you must answer it at last. If your children and servants grow up in the neglect of God, and pierce your hearts with those sorrows which such servants, and especially such children, are likely to occasion; if they raise profane and profligate families; if they prove the curse of their country, as well as the torment and ruin of those most intimately related to them; the guilt is in part yours, and, I repeat it again, you must answer it to God at the great day, that you have omitted the proper and appointed method of preventing such fatal evils. In the mean time you must answer the omission to your own conscience, which probably has not been easy in former days, and in future days may yet be more unquiet. Yet, sir, the memory of this address may continue to torment you, if it cannot reform you; and if you do not forsake the house of God, as well as exclude God and his worship from your own house, you will meet with new wounds; for new exhortations and admonitions will arm reflection with new reproaches. And in this uncomfortable manner you will probably go on, till what has been the grief and shame of your life, become the affliction of your dying bed; nor dare I presume to assure you that God will answer your last cries for pardon. The best you can expect, under the consciousness of this guilt, is to pass trembling to your final doom. But whatever that doom be, you must acquit the friend who has given you a faithful warning; and this address, transcribed as it were in the records of the divine omniscience, shall testify, that a matter of so great importance has not been kept out of your view, nor slightly urged on your conscience.

NOTES

MAN'S QUESTIONS & GOD'S ANSWERS

Am I accountable to God?
Each of us will give an account of himself to God. ROMANS 14:12 (NIV).

Has God seen all my ways?
Everything is uncovered and laid bare before the eyes of him to whom we must give account. HEBREWS 4:13 (NIV).

Does he charge me with sin?
But the Scripture declares that the whole world is a prisoner of sin. GALATIANS 3:22 (NIV).
All have sinned and fall short of the glory of God. ROMANS 3:23 (NIV).

Will he punish sin?
The soul who sins is the one who will die. EZEKIEL 18:4 (NIV).
For the wages of sin is death, but the gift of God is eternal life in Christ Jesus our Lord. ROMANS 6:23 (NIV).

Must I perish?
He is patient with you, not wanting anyone to perish, but everyone to come to repentance. 2 PETER 3:9 (NIV).

How can I escape?
Believe in the Lord Jesus, and you will be saved. ACTS 16:31 (NIV).

Is he able to save me?
Therefore he is able to save completely those who come to God through him. HEBREWS 7:25 (NIV).

Is he willing?
Christ Jesus came into the world to save sinners. 1 TIMOTHY 1:15 (NIV).

Am I saved on believing?
Whoever believes in the Son has eternal life, but whoever rejects the Son will not see life, for God's wrath remains on him. JOHN 3:36 (NIV).

Can I be saved now?
Now is the time of God's favor, now is the day of salvation. 2 CORINTHIANS 6:2 (NIV).

As I am?
Whoever comes to me I will never drive away. JOHN 6:37 (NIV).

Shall I not fall away?
Him who is able to keep you from falling. JUDE 1:24 (NIV).

If saved, how should I live?
Those who live should no longer live for themselves but for him who died for them and was raised again. 2 CORINTHIANS 5:15 (NIV).

What about death and eternity?
I am going there to prepare a place for you. I will come back and take you to be with me that you also may be where I am. JOHN 14:2-3 (NIV).

www.ingramcontent.com/pod-product-compliance
Lightning Source LLC
Chambersburg PA
CBHW020552030426
42337CB00013B/1070